CATS

Created by Gallimard Jeunesse
and Pascale de Bourgoing
Illustrated by Henri Galeron

A FIRST DISCOVERY BOOK

Cartwheel
·B·O·O·K·S· ™

SCHOLASTIC INC.
New York   Toronto   London   Auckland   Sydney

Here comes a cat,
creeping quietly on its
thickly padded paws.

The cats we keep
as pets are called
domestic cats.

Almost all cats have a coat of soft fur to
protect them and keep them warm.

The elegant Siamese has a
long, thin tail and blue eyes.

The Scottish-fold
has bent ears.
It is a breed developed in
Scotland in the 1960s.

What kind of mood is your cat in?
Look at his eyes, ears, and whiskers
to get some clues!

Cats love to sleep, day or night.
But at night, a cat can see better than you can.
Cats can't see colors, though — only shades of gray.
They hear very well, and can even point
one ear toward a sound to hear it better.

Peaceful   Angry   Frightened   Happy

In the dark, a cat's pupils become round
and open. In bright light,
they narrow to slits.

He's confident.

He's distrustful.

He's nervous.

Cats groom themselves
very carefully.
They lick themselves
clean from their heads
down to their tails.
Their tongues are
rough, like
sandpaper.

He stretches and feels good.

He's feeling affectionate.

You can be sure a cat is happy when it walks with its tail held high in the air.

A female can have as many as
six kittens in a litter.

Mother cats feed their kittens
until they are two months old.

When the kittens are tiny,
their mother carries them gently in her mouth.

When they are not busy sleeping or suckling,
what do kittens do? They play!

With their
powerful
muscles,

cats
can leap
very high.

and land on all
four paws. But if
they fall too far,
they *can* get hurt.

Cats use their
sharp claws
to climb high up
into trees.
If they fall,
cats try to twist
themselves around . . .

Cats' claws
are very sharp.
They can bare them
or pull them in
whenever they want.

A cat silently stalks its prey.
Then, suddenly, it
leaps forward and
seizes the animal
in its paws.

A cat has five toes on each
front paw, and four toes on each
hind paw. Spongy pads on the bottom
of each paw allow cats to move
without a sound.

Ocelots have particularly
lovely markings. No two
ocelots look the same.

The lynx lives in
northern forests,
and has a heavy
coat to protect it
from the cold.

All cats, big or small, are called felines.
Do you know the names of some of the
domestic cat's larger cousins in the wild?

The cheetah
is the fastest animal
in the world.

The lion has a thick,
shaggy mane.
The lioness
doesn't.

The jaguar is the largest
of the American wild cats.
It lives in the rain forests
of Central and South America.

The tiger is the biggest of all felines.
It is a fierce hunter, and lives in Asia.

We don't know when cats were first tamed,
but it might have been as long as
5,000 years ago. Ancient Egyptians
considered them sacred and
worshiped them.

Siamese cats once guarded royal palaces
and temples in Thailand.
But in Europe, in the middle ages,
people feared cats. Now they are
one of the most popular pets of all!

Titles in the series of *First Discovery Books:*

Airplanes and Flying Machines
Bears
Cats
Colors
The Earth and Sky
The Egg
Fruit
The Ladybug and Other Insects
The Tree
Weather

Library of Congress Cataloging-in-Publication Data available.

Originally published in France under the title LE CHAT by Editions Gallimard.

No part of this publication may be reproduced, in whole or in part, or stored in a retrieval system, or transmitted in any form or by any means, electronic, mechanical, photocopying, recording, or otherwise, without written permission of the publisher. For information regarding permission, write to Scholastic Inc., 730 Broadway, New York, NY 10003.

ISBN 0-590-45269-X

Copyright © 1989 by Editions Gallimard.
This edition English translation by Karen Backstein.
This edition American text by Karen Backstein.
All rights reserved. First published in the U.S.A. in 1992 by Scholastic Inc., by arrangement with Editions Gallimard.

CARTWHEEL BOOKS is a trademark of Scholastic Inc.

12 11 10 9 8 7 6 5 4 3   2 3 4 5 6 7/9

Printed in Italy by Editoriale Libraria

First Scholastic printing, September 1992